Divine cultured"

Glorified purity, integrity, honesty, benevolence, intelligent progressiveness
Predominantly confident, never swaying his life avoiding living in str fe
Mind is dynamite explosive like the knights, visualizing his concepts
Refraining from material objects, correcting teachers that's teaching us non-sense
A peak is what we've accomplished, a goodness that's keeping a healthy conscious
Immunity perfection of a blessing of reception in a reality of dominant lessons
That history's delivered us but the treacherous is infamous for dece t
That's why we can't meet self-defeat of a fetus retreat
Emcees that rhymes in high degrees cures mental disease eradicating greed
Underground rappers proved that they don't need to be on TV to gain notoriety
Because we have a variety of paralleled versatility, plus we have poetic chemistry
My diligence is vigilant of eloquent literature that describes life poet cally
I entertain my audience as I revolve while I evolve with wise attributions
To the people who never heard ideas that's new, so fresh and elusive
I'm over standing the days I observe, congruently being faithful because words are like birds
Because they apply to every living being, that's unseen or unheard

"Overcome blindness"

I construct the flow, most times is so prestigious but when I'm falling off
I'm fighting for my genius; writer's block got me thinking
Reading keeps me from sinking until my thoughts begin to deepen
Composing music for political reason to confront these dangerous demons who commit treason
Chauvinism speaks loudly when you're proud about your country but make sure you save the hungry
Humanitarian expansion across overseas educates people to want to help people to be free
Away from tragedy cause poor people are still starving but regardless
I'm going to make efforts to push harder, saving the generation from tropical storms of complication
And neglectful implication and lamentable condition with the intention of creating a vision
That's works more like an invention; I want to be sophisticated when it comes to making a difference
Without damage affliction, I am not looking for a sovereign; I'm looking for a truth doctrine
That's astronomical like stargaze; we have an unbearable wicked system that invades comfort of living
With politicians making bad decisions, denouncing interchangeable positions that could rejuvenate the earth
But all they want is a curse, they want our artist to deteriorate society and keep them from knowledge
Systematic destruction, indoctrinating the indigenous nemesis, critical division it's like a bad religion
Lack of distinction and bad behavior relinquishes humanity's kindness
Towards the persons of faith and warrant, we need to overcome blindness

"Culmination apotheosis"

Independent thinking saved me from indoctrination, I studied apotheosis so I can reach a culmination
No longer am I feeling desperate to want to become famous, is my life changing
Away from stress because my humility made me a huge success and now I have more than I have less
I underestimated the power of cultivation, used to feel like I was living in the dark ages
But now I'm now blessed living a healthy life avoiding the worst situations
My endowment to life is a positive contribution, uplifting the less fortunate is my contribution
To attain goals of merit, empowerment and global citizenship
Teaching the exact ways to motivate people who fail to penetrate minds and stimulate the times
Of uncertainty injustice, I pray for the poor and blind trying to find various ways to enlighten those
Who misunderstand life's identity, so they can be aware of imperative events that happens continuously
I want to impel people about how to live right and have fun
I personify humanity with persistent perseverance of integrity
Because I was born to be consistent, to speak to the gifted about revolutionizing living condition
The perspicuity of life believes in your dreams, doesn't anybody tell you different

"Industry truth"

Impurity is easy to emulate while righteousness is hard to obtain
The condition of this universe is hard to explain that's why it's hard to maintain
No one acknowledges precautions of a crime before they commit it
So many ending up in prison making the wrong decisions
You thought revolution was dead, well I'm delivering it
Hip Hop today is an embarrassment to all of our living golden age legends
Circus of clowns with no substance staying repetitive
What is up with our lyricist who can't get any deals?
They rather have mass appeal than have an artist that's real
Intelligent art is what I feed with all of the knowledge I conceal
So many can't get ahead in life their steady losing their minds
And people who try to make it are left behind
The new world order establishment has got our brains exploding
The whole world has awoken because our freedom was stolen

"The needy"

We've awakened the giant from illusions including the disillusioned producing intelligent fusion
My magnetic mind is never losing; excuses are tools of incompetence to stop progression
Exceptional faith is what I'm testing coming with a plan of aggression to invest with digression
I'm my own friend I don't need acceptance in this game of trickery, dishonesty and deception
With no exception I respect what is given but when the universe is crumbling it makes me more driven
Optimism, opportunity, peace love and unity is what I'm influencing for every community
I want to ignite people with my passion, enlighten bright minds and unify peoples of all kinds
My goal is to be the greatest role model of all time, be a hero to most and never commit a crime
Be a devotion to human salvation, I want to outshine my own mind using my creative innovation
I want Paradise to be everybody's home and let everyone feel like they are not alone in every nation
I want every soul healed and healthy so they can live in amazement because too many people die in the struggle
Too many people get caught up in the dying of trouble; it's survival that keeps us from the dangerous huddle
And the dangerous storms and dangerous conditions we see on the norm
So let's extinguish this extravaganza, so when the sick is suffering let's tell them we got the healing power answer
Why is propaganda propagated by folks who could create change?
It's turning to the point where they want unlawful acts to stay the same
I'm not saying that the older generation is greedy
But some neglect the poor to suffer in devastation and abandon the needy

"Flow poem"

Come and try to master this like a classic disk, my abstract rhymes be disastrous like I'm monstrous
So marvelous, I keep my flow gritty with wit as I describe how to emcee to my peeps while these metaphors flip
Stupid creation translating true greatness like a poetic wordsmith, I publish it like a newspaper
Maneuvering with alliteration, asking my opponent who's got the most flavors? Who's greater?
I got unwavering support from those who dug my style; they say you're so good your name should be freestyle
Although I need work at my freestyles, I still manage to rip miss taking poetic hip hop to new heights
I am the prototype without the need for new hype, using insightful rhymes to drop knowledge insight
Making infectious connections giving these rookie emcees a lesson, I practice with aggression
My upgrading and my investments is what I'm testing, leaving my critics silent with no bad impression
I train my mind with optimistic philosophies, full-filling my prophecies
To reach apotheosis so I can create happiness for everybody
Including those who's not in tune or satisfied with reality
That's how I want people to remember me
The one's who's educated the world through rhyming at high degrees
The one who kept it real as a raw emcee
The one who's viewed as a great person to the people I meet

Escape of the dumb down illusion"

Educational nourishment is what I feed the nation with embellishment, visual concepts
Lyrical aspect, I teach them humanity, how to operate successfully
Achieving their dreams so peep's can stand on their destiny
I preach human salvation, Hip Hop humanitarian
Knowledge philanthropist, donating lyrical excellence
Creative remedy to solve the community, establishing thesis
Establishing unity, influential sanctity for betterment of unity
Masterful poetry with intelligent imagery
I take it back to the golden age days like the symphony
I got nothing to lose against these arrogant emcees
Who spews Incredulous stories about how they run the streets
It's easy to make good music without saying anything
But where's the message of gratification, the truth telling
Because lack an empty disk of lack of truth is what you're selling
You don't have to be rebellious starting a violent revolution
But those who are scared to tell the truth is selling immutable confusion
An ignorant mindset creates a dumb down illusion

"Change"

Orchestrated propaganda machines organize fail systems to destroy labor unions
With degenerate mechanisms meaning that they monopolize the tax system
Causing stagnation and obstructionism and enjoy creating working class victims
Government manipulation's got them terrified; some doctors discriminate against
patients who are paralyzed
Police are murdering the harmless and the homeless are suffering
Bankers created collateral damage and economic destruction
Conspiracy theorist are waking up the world from trouble and revolution is the answer
I'd rather die from natural causes than die from cancer, there is no equilibrium
We're all experiencing oppression, although we are recovering from the great recession
I have propagated investments to save the world from calamity
And save these activist from reaching insanity, I have hope teaching people to use it
And excessive its audacity, my vitality is as strong as my tenacity
No more procedural tragedies and disparity, divisive complexity
I have faith in believing in people for more equality even if one disagrees with me
Music is charity and a blessing to those going through the pain
I promise you a difference of change and a future of change

"Lyrical operation"

Lyrical operation conjugation raw translation to transform the universe for universal
changes
Providing intelligent language illuminating the darkness, stop influencing imitation
Grand of knowledge of greatness to avoid those wanting to strangle it, preventing
endangerment
Pandemonium of vulgar content leads to distortion, extorting the image of Hip Hop
The lack of purity nowadays in mainstream spreads non-stop, it's a shame how some
flop
But I remain educating them with moral principles like theosophy
Healing the universe with therapeutic psychology using a righteous philosophy
They dominating cooperative media like technocracy, cats flow sloppy
And no one's practicing properly; it's appalling how most don't even take themselves
seriously
We need to embolden those to think diligent and stay vigilant
When it comes to protecting my rights, I remain militant

"Divine cultured II"

I am not buying this degeneration; I'm about educating the masses with pure inspiration
The game is going through a plague and I'm here to be its salvation
I'm well-behaved in the sense of living righteous spitting without hesitation
I feed you parables of truth, no coincidence, I be the image of the magnificent
God's presence cause he showed me the light of heaven
And I've became accustomed to his word and he's my medicine
I discipline youth with promise, seeking Jesus the prophet
Studying the facts about ancient knowledge, my soul is free from bondage
I give astonishing intimacy of communicating peacefully
The diplomatic force that saves life from misleading infantry
I keep minds stabilized so they won't suffer from any harmful tragedy
Although people practice malfunction, I destroy the infidelity
Perpetually I seek my inner peace so it can keep my mind at ease
Keep the environment free so we can live nice and happily
By transforming myself so I can change the world to live in serenity

"Hope For All": (2012)

The economy is suffering; we're losing all our soldiers in war
We want money, we're greedy for more
Nuclear chemical corruption, weapons of mass destruction
Veterans are sick in the brain like spontaneous combustion
Markets are stumbling, we're crashing, and we're fumbling
The Government is fronting, he ain't doing nothing
We need better discussion, let's start the revolution
Let's end all of the sexual schemes and prostitution
We need a solution to this non-sense, let's abolish racism and hate
Reveal the secrets before it's too late
Communication is the key to respect, we need more dialogue
Be careful on the road, never drive through the fog
We need clean energy and air so let's install
Be careful what you eat from the stores they have recalls
I spread knowledge and hope for all
So don't fall prey to the God who helps you through it all

"Lyrical project"

Transitional progress, transformation process, lyrical prowess being astute as I'm dominant
The novelist, poetic lyricist keeping his message in depth, it's so dense that's why they say it's so tense
At an expense, so elusive with intelligent fusion far from dumb down illusion
He preaches activism salvation that terminates execution overseas a compassionate degree
Over freedom at ease, cleaning up the streets the branches and trees
Visual conceptualization is my specialty, grand communication, making an impact without being ostentatious
I'm thankful and so gracious, obliged, grateful to be alive, we struggle to survive that's how we thrive
I analyze with dynamic perception to mobilize the game through intellectual facts and then I use introspection
Never neglecting the secret weapon to clean up the disease so I can cure the infection
I fight to be good so I can earn critical reception
Talent supersedes life, art imitates life, hype imitates entertainment or should I say it is influenced by
Overrated inoculations usually there's a conversation about who is the next who, the next prospect of lyrical objects
But on empirical logic, those who dominate go the hardest, regardless of skepticism, we build empires
Winning awards and accolades, ripping mics, setting stages on fire

"World prison"

One world government domination, ungodly occupation, devilish occupation, false characterization
Everyone dying overseas with their legs amputated and dis-configured and discombobulated
Death orchestrated civil war organizations, misconstrued concepts, and poverty stricken projects
That's my devotion of the world is to be the object, no more army is a salvation, dangerous demonstration
Heads severed on the battlefield severely, miserable facilitated calamity that's why I scream it's all insanity
Lack of vanity, it's like war destroyed humanity, immutable capacity due to tumultuous tragedies
Destroying industries, laying off companies, we live in a society where it's hard to achieve
Misconceived truth, mass deception, economy stagnated by bad investments, ridiculousness
Despite this I haven't lost hope in my vision, so we ain't accepting this depopulation
Or this homogenized milk they selling, that's stuff will leave your liver swelling
GMO Mechanics will leave a hole in your heart, open collapsed immunity
But most importantly we can be healthy by in taking our food source carefully
No more fighting for oil and resources, let's cool down the war motive tension
And let's defeat the defeatist attitude and the dysfunctional political system
And stop the world from heinous crimes before it turns into a world prison

"Power of human transformation"

The revolutionary fights for freedom eradicating his demons, saving humanity from danger
He inextricably makes peace with the Middle East with stability cooling down the anger
He never mismanages diplomatic obligations because the world wanted justice like the emancipation proclamation
Now we have elitist who's segregating us using wealth division, criminals trying to supply us with fluoride prescriptions
But our motive is to do about this is overrule them, be like a rebel when it comes to a genocidal system
It's so sadistic and twisted how they begin to petrify, why don't we exercise liberty instead of imitating division
And strange behavioral patterns that ruins our chances of change, the system wants us to be the same
We keep on dying, employees keep getting fired, and we're living in a world of poverty
Most people nowadays are unacquainted to the confusion and dysfunction
The seriousness that keeps the world from loving one another
See the universe needs to be treated like a good seed
But they want to destroy it because they feel life ain't what it seems
So where's the love of what happened to living by God's principle
I'm sure anybody don't want to leave the earth with a negative residuals
Let's grow accustomed to enlightenment and incite more people to co right
And live a sustainable life, educate every, mind, no more ignorant information
Beyond historical evidence scientifically we can all achieve the power of human transformation

"Life"

Tranquility's hard to find like atheist who can't convert to religion, so much political division
Racial tension, we need a revision, I can't believe people are so obsessed with death and pessimism
Physically we're getting sicker and sicker, discriminate laws keep of color in misery
I wish I was happier, it feels like those who claim that they are happy be still caught in misery
Even the nicest person who show kindness got anger inside of them, it's so sad
People seem like their never willing to change, on a different day they act the same
It's like some people despise change, all I'm praying for is miracles to keep me satisfied
Because I aren't satisfied until the universe is revolutionized, a gift seems no longer a surprise
That's why I'm hurting inside; I'm struggling for enjoyment in this life
When people act disobedient and lack purity, you know something ain't right
We imitate what we watch, read and listen to, influenced by these wicked doctrines
Since we were born and trouble is what we got into and look where it got us
I guess people ain't born to live a perfect life, too much pain and strife
I don't know what to do I tried to make the best out of my life
But I guess not because I'm still dealing with obstacles in my life

"Sovereign emcee"

Never take an emcee for granted even if he's unskilled
Never sell your soul in this business for some mass appeal
The truth is never hard to reveal once you've captured it
Like conspiracy theorist that expose scare tactics and things that are graphic
By these wicked politicians with insane dominions
Destroying their domain using extortion and fallacy opinions
So much derision, people tortured worse than feudalism
Division, lack of will power, hours wasted, cities devastated
Terrorism, military operation, malfunction, citizen corruption
Environmental destruction, so much lust for fame and money
Fear and rejection, misconceived ideology, misconception, crookec policies
Unconventional mentality commodities, extremism, lack of wisdom
Freedom is what I envision so I can have a vision
Although I embrace uber optimism, I accept constructive criticism
Feeble minded people get it together to many criminals
Sitting here in prison, they want to rule the world to make a profit
The super-rich want to monopolize the government in Washington
Although I support government, I still remain sovereign

"Off the wall lyricism"

I write rhyme in complex context, indistinguishably ill, my flow is real as it gets
It's too phenomenal, don't mean to be braggadocios but the vocab is ferocious moving
your brain like hypnosis
Undeniably nice as I entice crowds, bewilder and astound, leave you frustrated by
literacy compounds
It's too magnetic, too hardcore for you'll synthetic clowns; I pull mics and show you'll
lyrical aesthetic
Booming harder than surround sounds, impressive diction like verbal athletics using
poetic acuity, so articulate
Influencing golden age lyricism, so advanced with wordplay, viciously convincing with
the wisdom
Astronomically compelling with the invention, invincible, I'm capable of being the
greatest of similes and syllables
I rejuvenate the game, making the plague obsolete with my dynamic language, scientific
dialect
Intelligent enough to complete to deplete all of the confusion and fiction on this
industrialized set
Of commercialism, dedicated to those who feed trash to the nation, this is an intellectual
invasion
To all these misleading radio stations who negatively influences the younger generation
They steady jeopardizing all of the future generations, destroying the culture
Infiltrating the minds of those who avoid lyrical education, leading our kids in the wrong
direction facing temptation
Making the game less innocent and more ignorant with evil obligations
It's seems like you'll forgot about the basics, we've been teaching you'll for ages

"Heart"

My flow be the agility, my rhythm is the mobility, my dialectic frame be the energy that delivering me
Visually I seek knowledge at high degrees, until no one sees any more lack of skills in me
Fundamentally exceptional, the diehard intellectual, highly respected and acceptable
I'm well-loved on the streets and hardly ever ridiculed, living by a messiah's principle
If I had a lot of money I wouldn't act as if I'm invincible because I'm not above the law
And I'm not a hog who doesn't care about those who fall, I'm about saving lives that's how I ball
All of you'll who dethrone yourselves by dissatisfaction, I'm going to let you know that God's saving all
Righteously gifted is how I present myself and my demeanor, I am the ultimate dreamer who's purified cleaner
Than the negative sinners that's pessimistic extremist, forget money and jewels, I captivate those with presence
I'm going to put an end to those who tries to make efforts to get the revolutionary beheaded
So don't begrudge me for doing the right thing, justice and expansion of equality let's freedom ring
I try not to be obscene when my mind is kicking crazy thoughts, to walk with Jesus there's no cost
There is no turning back and there is no holding back
Even I died and failed and came back from a failed cardiac
There's no way of eradication to nullify love and compassion, you can't rid of that
And there's something inside of us that we don't lack and that's heart

"Artist"

I engrave futuristic design with rhymes of steel without the need of mass appeal or no major deal
Going aggressive with progression giving the youth a lesson, compose with originality
You know what's real, no imitation insight, words of depth with insight
Complex lyricism takes me to unbelievable heights, my words are melodic
The message is sporadic above and beyond average and my mind stays static
I try harder than most emcees that pick up the pen, not to brag
But my talent acts with proof and I never pretend
Big up to those who send a deep message to the universe
Especially the rap world that went through identity issues of a major curse
From these major companies that neglected the artist

"Facade"

Condescension on the newscast stations, violent facade and hatred, planet shifting into a complex
Digital Satan matrix, they try to kill the revolutionary taking down civ l liberties
A nation with 900 military bases has gone through misery
Execution operations overseas is growing frantic like the plague
Cancerous diseases deadlier than HIV and Aids
Trillions of dollars wasted and stolen, my brain frame is frozen
By these battlefield depleted uranium explosives
Nearly 9 million casualties, the world is living in agony
What happened to the bible telling you to turn the other cheek?
Jesus wouldn't fight in war and neither would God
Just by thinking about this has got me struck like a lightning rod
I'm brainstorming for important information to gather
Because my mind is getting scattered and the condition of this worlc is getting sadder
Some of my dreams shattered and splattered
So I maneuver like a master, the evil is disastrous

Lyrical operation"

Lyrical operation conjugation raw translation to transform the universe for universal changes
Providing intelligent language illuminating the darkness, stop influencing imitation
Grand of knowledge of greatness to avoid those wanting to strangle it, preventing endangerment
Pandemonium of vulgar content leads to distortion, extorting the image of Hip Hop
The lack of purity nowadays in mainstream spreads non-stop, it's a shame how some flop
But I remain educating them with moral principles like theosophy
Healing the universe with therapeutic psychology using a righteous philosophy
They dominating conspiracy media like technocracy, cats flow sloppy
And no one's practicing properly; it's appalling how most don't even take themselves seriously
We need to embolden those to think diligent and stay vigilant
When it comes to protecting my rights, I remain militant

"Rebuild it"

They got us in a fix its manipulation Luciferian flames burning in the world's destruction
Times running out I keep on punching until my revolutions achieved
It feels like I lost air to breath, I'm holding on to my self esteem
So many perpetrators got away with worshiping Satan in high degrees
It needs to be distinguished before we can't answer
I'm talking about these culprits, the world's number one cancer
Who believe elitism is right but we prove them its injustice
Governmental dysfunction, congressional corruption
Filibusters and gridlock holding the country in hostage
That's why the President's resorts to executive orders to stop the monster
So he can free those who's hurting in bondage
Gerrymandering politicians be stealing elections
Overseas ammunition, explosives and weapons, purity desolation
And promiscuity is being syndicated and now we got perverted shows on radio stations
Their poisoning the minds of our children
Ever since Adam and Eve we pledged to change the earth so let's rebuild it

"Positivism"

It's my desire that drives me
It's my commitment to fulfill my dreams
It's my exuberance, the confidence that makes me do creative things
It's my passion that makes people believe in me
It's my determination that keeps me doing things willfully
I take life seriously, I think independently
I dignify one's integrity, the ones who show respect to me
I diminish all the evil that's inside of me by operating peacefully
I promote a life of fairness teaching people how to live decently
Even though I'm a bit of extreme when it comes to being clean
I take away the infamy that's in the industry
I propagate the laws of living in harmony
I diversify cultural acceptance by uniting people in high degrees
I educate my mind to be free from the drama that I sometimes witness
I invest in self-development relying on it because it provides a vision
If more people want a difference in life, they must change how they're living

"Ancient Civilization"

Militarism, war occupation, one world government domination, we need to reinvent this broken nation, end every casualty, take it back to 1776, a healthy economy with no debt to fix
Elite controlled organization, fraternities owned by Freemasons, indoctrination education
Negative vibrations, newscasters lying, coastal fractured by disasters, evil globalization
Institutions, misguided sheep are blinded by the media, denying factual proof
Dumbing down the youth, misconceptions of religions and its indigenous origin of where it came from, all religions have truth; I'm still waiting for them to bring home the troops
I'm trying to be awake so I can be astute; the truth movement is what I salute
Shut off the TV and read a book like Technique said
And stop letting false ideas ruin your head
Establish your own life until its right and never fall prey like a victim
Because when you fall prey like a victim you'll have it harder than a prisoner
Open your eyes and see the world for what it is without fate
And put a squeeze to all these criminals before it's too late
Fight against corruption and injustice, overthrow the wicked system
Design the future with promise and free the ones who are innocent

"Global empowerment"

Exceptional progression, I'm manifesting the truth to save your spirit
Equalizing humanity with my uplifting lyrics
Proving anyone can achieve the impossible with opportunity
I invest in merit preventing the youth from crumbling
Read factual information, upgrading education
Optimistically influencing those to eradicate invalid information
Self-worth and encouragement, an urgency to change is what I preach
Keep a positive motive help up in reach
The protagonist never retreats or faces defeat
Making sure that my message resonates among the strong and weak
Concrete brainstorming thoughts kills deception
And also media's injections, no more poison in being effective
No more bad reflection or bad reception

"Revitalization of the industry"

Musical profundity profligates the crisis of the industry, I be the preacher
Revealing truth as I'm viewed as the Hip Hop extremist
I elucidate it to those who misunderstands the art of emceeing
I refine every evil entity such as symbolism and satanic rituals
I'm trying to get the youth to understand that some corporations are owned by criminals
And how the now these they trying to devalue the dollar
And how the revolutionary is ridiculed
I am the visionary who speaks with tact sending positive vibration
Talking to those who misinterpret the facts, the real Glen is back
I'm steady searching for deep information; I got a lot of things to learn
I feel behind but my message of hope never burns
It seems like we're failing at succeeding in advancement, believing everything we hear
From the news squandering chances to take the opportunity
I'm all about peace and unity, the love for every culture
And community, I know I don't have a lot to say
Except have a different objective for agenda on a different day
I came to change the world; I didn't come here for play

"Think freely"

Blasphemy, hypocrisy, lies and false analogy
 So much misinformation, media speaking illogically
End all of the violence, end all of the hatred, and win over Satan
This is my clear demonstration, no more problems to be facing
No more opposition, positive decisions over bad intentions
My vision is what will save humanity from collision because unity is what I envision
For a brighter future to restore the world's image because war is coming to its ending
Whenever I sin I ask god for forgiveness, practice my word to live a life that sinless
I'm beginning to see the world rise up, they said enough is enough
We've reached a time to save those who were headed towards hell
One place to avoid before you die so you can live alive and well
The second place to avoid is a place where they keep you locked in a cell
Once place you want to be at is heaven, gates where you live in paradise for eternity
We need to erase the negative words from the dictionary
And influence those who write and read to think positively
Take away every form of pain, relieve our minds and think freely

"Penmanship"

I walk a straight line pavement on the way to reach my destination dropping lyrical bombs
Without hesitation, I drop biblical truth like revelation, I trace like an oasis
As my mind is attached to the adjacent field of intellectual conversation
We're lacking substance on radio stations, lack of cadence and alliteration
Some cats be coming off as simplistic, incoherent and inarticulate it's so ridiculous
We're offering a message but they didn't listening, my heart is yearning
For the world to be educated and more sophisticated, we need to exercise lyricism
Like a gymnasium, we need industrious scholars that's not concerned with making dollars
You don't need to brag, you're already honored for your hardships and winning over your struggles, just because he's popular don't mean that you have to go commercial
Just inoculate incorporate innocence in this industrialized industry of computerized programming system of ignorance, if you're rich why don't you give back to those who are penniless, stop the selfishness, why are negatively influencing kids?, fix that and step up your penmanship

"Unlimited potential"

Mass murder occupations and secret organizations are controlled by CIA operations
Trillions of dollars wasted, massive amounts of people dying in war without peace
Society is held under government officials and thieves, colonizing so many countries
Over 900 military bases and 300 territories, by different faces
The youth is struggling, educational system pummeling
Power misused and abused by tragedy's procedure
The student fails to challenge the teacher
Jobs aren't paying us enough and schools are getting weaker
Hard workers are discredited, they got money laundering embezzlement
Embedded and forbidden chapters of masters of deception
Tamper and defeat the demographic calculation system to steal an election
My battleground states voted for democracy, not false hypocrisy
My ideology is to save people from suffering overseas
With a qualification that's related to learning in high degrees
If only you can see what I can see, unlimited potential

"American Obligation"

Theoretical defines America's system, I was meant to change the world not to die in a prison
Communicating between people's to save the planet from nuclear corruption
But these veterans are suffering from spontaneous combustion, what's missing?
A transformation cycle to illuminate the universe without destructior
A movement has begun to stop bombing and missile heat seeking
Without preaching there is no teaching without good there is any evil
But my main goal is to kill these decriminalized demons
Releasing the lion and the beast to expand history
My obligation is not to traumatize
Because the last thing I want to go through is being criticized

"World of trouble"

It's sickening to see people suffering severely with poverty and sickness
Homelessness and people struggling to open a business
So many people blinded by living in illusions, what fruit are we producing
The media feeding us mad confusion, politicians' feeding us excuses
How can we enable the right people to serve our interest?
Without being guided by crooks and dissidents, lack of freedom as-semblance
The food that they supply us with got us shooting some insulin
We're overshadowed by overrules and selfishness, they violating our rights
With unethical laws, unjust society, judicial system flawed
Some people looked down upon; elitism is getting worse, intimidation by the
government
Against the people and now our nation's hurt, the only thing that can stop us is if we
commerce
That's why I put what's important first; we got people who want us in the dirt
What happened to a free society, where we can live in joy and comfort?
I guess we nearly have to kill ourselves to work for what we deserve

"Heart"

My flow be the agility, my rhythm be the mobility, my dialectic frame be the energy that's delivering me
Visually I seek knowledge at high degrees until no one sees any more lack of skills in me
Fundamentally exceptional the diehard intellectual, highly respected and acceptable
I'm well-loved on the streets and hardly ever ridiculed, living by a messiah's principle
If I had a lot of money, I would act as if I'm invincible because I'm not above the law
And I'm not a hog who doesn't care about one's who fall, I'm about saving lives that's how I ball
All of yawl who dethrone yourselves by dissatisfaction, I'm going to et you know that God is saving all
Righteously gifted is how I present myself and my demeanor, I am the ultimate dreamer who's purified cleaner
Than the negative sinners that's pessimistic extremist, forget money and jewels
I can captivate those with presence; I put an end to those who makes efforts that try to get the revolutionary beheaded
So begrudge me for doing the right thing, justice and expansion of equality let's freedom ring
I try not to be obscene when my mind is kicking crazy thoughts, to walk with Jesus there is no cost
There is no turning back and there is no holding back
Even if I died and came back from a failed cardiac
There's no eradication for love you can't get rid of that
And there's something inside of all of us that we don't lack and that's heart

"Determination"

Lack of righteousness will lead you to the path of wrong decisions
Ungodly acts like drugs and violence defines bad living
That's why I keep my mind acquainted to reading God's power of knowledge
I had enough of setbacks that's why I'm free from bondage
Focused on his opportunity, he gives will to reach successes and the merit of unity
There's undeniable evidence of miracles that people saw
I always dreamed about living life without a single flaw
No matter how much the devil tries to tempt me
My goodness of my actions left his soul empty
Because I understood that he despised me from day one
And hated everything from the beginning, my struggle came to an ending
After the lord's soul delivered me and my now my soul is fortified intrinsically
So now I'm reaching my destination to get my education
Declining every offer from Satan outshining him with my determination

www.ingramcontent.com/pod-product-compliance
Lightning Source LLC
LaVergne TN
LVHW091211080426
835509LV00006B/947